You Don't Know My Story

A Teaching Book for Parents of Autistic Kids

Elise R. Johnston

tellwell

Tellwell Talent
www.tellwell.ca

ISBN
978-0-2288-0651-6 (Paperback)

Preface

Despite many great days, I suspect others don't know
the extra struggles I've had, watching my child grow.

I cry at frustrations and worries. It feels so unfair.
Can I get what we need? Beyond a hope and a prayer ...

But I've learned that my experiences over the years
are familiar to parents who've shed similar tears.

So smile at common challenges, offer an ear or a shoulder.
Let's support and help each other as our kids get older.

In the following pages, I share the calming of my thoughts,
reducing my stress, massaging out emotional knots.

My hope is that you too can lay down in bed
to slumber well, resting chaos that spins in your head.

Elise

Overwhelmed and under-supported, I'm always so tired.

How can I go on, unsure what to do, my patience expired?

Will it always be so, images of a 'normal' child broken?

Aspirations shift, with worries and fears unspoken.

I remind myself of ways that I am blessed,

that regardless of circumstances, I do try my best.

Even though at times, that seems not enough,

I will strive again tomorrow. I gotta be tough.

I try not to be rude when friends offer a 'helpful tip'

against my over-managing, over-protective grip.

"What happens when you let go?", "He's fine", "Let him be!"

Like I have to explain, he's not manipulating me.

I cover up well. You don't see how I'm stressed,

trying to manage through my life's constant test.

Know that each child-parent bond is unique.

What works for you, may not for us. I'm not just weak!

I hate that errands and shopping are such a trial,

my kid with sensory overload at every aisle.

I try to avoid meltdowns and embarrassing scenes

but that's not always easy, by any means!

You don't know my story; I'm doing my best.

You don't understand how he's different from the rest.

I wouldn't create this situation if I had a choice.

We'll be gone from here soon and you can rejoice.

I especially hate when others' reactions add to my grief,
like their annoyance will solve things. Is that their belief?
I suffer through outings including long-distance flights,
restraining my child only strengthen his fights.

Please don't judge, criticise, or react severely.
We're not trying to disturb you, I promise sincerely!
I reject others' problems; they don't belong to me.
This too shall pass. Breathe: one ... two ... three.

As the target of outbursts, I'm often being hit,

also kicked, pinched, scratched, punched and bit.

Though I've never yet been in any real danger,

how does 'pinned to the ground' look to a stranger?

I don't see that fighting back with force is right.

It adds to the stress, try as one might

to 'discipline' with aggression or even to remove

a cherished item. What does that prove?

Responding with unconditional love can't be wrong

but shows my child that I'm there all along.

I've had doubts about school, how they deal with his chants,
his unusual behaviour and wetting his pants.
I want him safe and cared for by teachers who are trained.
Ideally, he's stimulated and happy, not bullied or strained.

I'll keep searching for services and activities to help us:
alternative healers, diet, or meds? Much to discuss.
I'll never say what my child will not be able to do.
The future is not predetermined. I believe this to be true.

I'm wary of family gatherings and holidays;

no one particularly understanding of our ways.

Rituals and expectations add to our stress:

when to be where, what to eat, how to dress?!

I allow myself to stand back or pull away.

If that's what we need, please hear what I say.

We'll join when we can, do understand

we can't always come through exactly as planned.

My other child suffers in various ways
alongside my efforts to give special days.
Needing her to be patient, helpful, independent too,
she can't be responsible for what he might do.

I love you so much, aware of the extra burden
that you carry, unrequested, undeserved for certain.
I'll stay aware of your needs. I"ll do my part
to keep eyes open, ears, mind and heart.

Lucky my spouse is supportive, tender yet strong.

Though not without arguments, don't get me wrong!

Too bad we barely get quality alone time

to act out a 'perfect couple' paradigm.

I recall the excitement we had at the start,

I won't let parenting pull us apart.

I'll try to listen well and speak very clearly.

I need you as much as I love you dearly.

Conclusion

I permit myself to share the weight on my chest.

It brings some relief, but still I need rest.

So at the end of the day, as I fall into bed,

I calm my mind, the worries in my head.

I focus on my breath, follow it, slow and deep.

dissolving tensions within, helping me sleep.

Once I'm relaxed, I do some visualisations

of happy scenes, or say my affirmations:

   I maintain all hope as it helps me cope.

     (repeat 10x)

   I hold on to DREAMS; life's not as bad as it seems!

     (repeat 10x)

Resources for Stress Management Techniques

My Website www.AlivewithElise.com Expounds on this 3-pronged approach which has helped me deal with the stresses of life in positive ways. I've added a page on autism to share video examples, links and helpful information.

Mindful Living techniques:

DEEP BREATHING is the number one de-stressor for numerous reasons.

Mindfulness, meditation and visualisation can be easy, worthwhile exercises for many whereas others may prefer journaling as a way of releasing bad energy.

Sharing with others who can relate is very helpful and there are countless Facebook groups if you don't have other parents in your area.

Sound therapy is soothing: music or nature sounds can help you relax or sleep.

EFT is 'Tapping' on your own acupressure points with guided affirmations.

CBT and Neuro-Linguistic Therapy has been used for people with PTSD and addictions, but also works well by generally reducing negative thought patterns.

Cold Laser / Infra-red therapy is also being used for PTSD as anti-anxiety help.

Mindful Eating:

By reducing sugars, processed and artificial ingredients while increasing healing foods such as greens, teas, spices, anti-oxidants, pro- and pre-biotics, your body will reduce inflammation and balance hormones such as cortisol. All your systems start to function better without the toxins and you will be amazed at how much better you feel and can deal with problems. (This is especially true for your child as well! Going Gluten-free was life-changing for us.)

Mindful Movement:

With even a little bit of gentle exercise or even just stretching, the blood flow will give you more energy and improve both your immunity and mood.

I love dancing and yoga, as well as enjoying the outdoors with my family, but do whatever you enjoy. Ideally you can have some fun physical time with your child(ren) too.

CPSIA information can be obtained
at www.ICGtesting.com
Printed in the USA
LVHW070420220319
611486LV00001B/3/P